My Earliest Person

My Earliest Person

Jennifer Soong

    Nothing gets past me now
except your being everything
       beyond my love:
light, low granules of it clasped
       upon a lake. A natural
starting point, in which I find

       you cannot end up at,   anymore. So a person
       unsteadily transplanted across
       the slow flowing, to say

       beyond my love is the world of my love,
to mean: I have not buried anything in words
       you may rest in and lift out
       if not life, wherever you are.

The lake is even larger than I imagined.
       The photos mean nothing, I delete
the evidence to this poem, but it is

       to be felt, not pictured, the argument,
let by us to become it:
       Can't you see? I'm certain you do already,
glimmering in the gift that we know less
       than what we are.

I am let down by the world
             nothing turns out
to be you. east street
     past the damp dim tunnel
is my throat
       left saying your name

       is language mad or work towards
perfection

what happened to us   as adults

to punch   stars
       their discs   way out
the space
free of their burning

o it is never and night and what one is
is useful to one's own heart

       the world manages
to behold my irrelevance and flowing of gust's
green heart
callous of browning buds

my breasts mumble   none of us is spared
embodying

the world can be found applying itself

       where time's enough
  the feeling frays

Often I feel without reason
        in this arrangement
between myself

     whose shadows away
deluxe clouds
  heartwork the
     product of a funk

do I do freely what I cannot happily?

     helpless in this we are

my heart is shady in this work of
  other-living
        gladdened
on behalf of nothing

I was referred to you by my past

am let out occasionally by
                      words

    clouds leave the
sun   o praise and quiet to the one
  who leaves a quiet path

I can love you

love exhausts my
                judgmental nature

     untie these hands of yours

      Love inverts the secret
      overhanging the river's buccal
plane, as obvious
      as what comes to us, least true
in words. Feeling gets to

      the top beyond
   staying where it least
      can be: the hill   disembarks
with tears. It comes

with being around you again, the trivia
      weeping with
importance, the oxbow lake with

      thick grinding lanes. To able
      the moveable globes
contrive with love feeling so

real, it no longer matters the word it
comes in. A clumsy
      one upside-down

like a river of open clouds. Open
      and we pass not words but life.

      Every attempt, now
      is an attempt at everything
      up till these stars of snow. That's what

      I can't say without knowing
to sing with different words the same song
      is a kind of death. And this is what

      I continuously don't have,
      the words, to say.   Days continue
      to appear and push

back dawn, as February lays off
      and spring flowers, surround

      whoever we were. Years
coping on foot, in the city of jacked
      stars. Any thought is a
      miracle.   You skived those trees to be

      held in. I'd like to save some of
      it for you, whatever falls
      out of your comfort.

Thus far steps just past us, at most
      each thing still existing, speechless.
      Light reflects off cones. Where one
continues, I don't want

back dawn. Only a leaden path
      petals distant enough to summon,
      hills of snow.

By tendrils darkless days
dim this slope's union of
earth's green fur: one capsule

per "little block heart"
drinks and is gentle again.
Under pollarded trees

earth laminated by light.
Much as it is mine
my forehead close to you

to touch. Sleeveless tendrils
soaking in your tulip-gathering
whichever willing course.

Snow done falling fans down trees
cars with their humps of snow. What it
announces I position myself next
to, a flock of cold one can feel.
By nature we fear change. But what is quiet, barely
there in us that learns.

And the flowers. "how happy I am
they're alive"—

      Let us, when they're at last
revealed lose our days we live out
        as love. What I give away by
merely imbuing into it more of,

          than what is not myself. A place

     where cold flurries peter out of you
     a trace in the wording of how
much we care to let it, into that place.

     When you reach out with your dope careless
     when flurries pulp the stalwartness
     of your being I happen to be looking for

And it gets to me, the way everything
     now gushes from and towards the
way I come to feel
     known. You ask me if I'd ever go
the distance. You aren't

       where you used to be, but it is merely

my own hope that you ask. Increasingly
    the way of return feels
    shorter. We don't go that way.

Take to me as I desire. That
        which depends: love
I'm hopeful about, as a thing
people can imagine

        speaking to you   of. Back

from the pool, in the lay
        of your land, of this world
where the flooded meadow, the
vacancy of bird I let teem

                a few zucchini
    flowers, celebration
        flutes, hold these, all
  sorts of things...

"I see, not feel, how beautiful they are"
to you till I don't have to
                anymore. Think

apricity. Think *election*. Think *but I
can't*. It's hard to turn

away from joy. Some words
come together to flow and migrate north.
If you can meet me where I'm at

*which bits of this
crackle in the mouth
doesn't matter*

It's what can still come of this   I'm after

Swathed in light earliest half of morn
falling out the gut of
days, unlined pastures
lax bluish left to
bleed, beauty rest assured, nine
out of ten employees in this poem
can't be seen,
my headache employed in a
skin of white: a hard fog craving to break this
temple on.

Where does anything
I say go? I am
halved into muteness
by light
        so far miscarried into
pastures, lays out fast and slow my
confusions. My heart can't say anymore
a child is good, wretchedness
enough, or if the darker lights
shall get out from that
without becoming violence itself.

Absorbed the light, trees totter
upon this swab of land.
For each part of me, let there truly be
no equivalent in it to correspond to the work,
let it be of another place.

Under deflected commons
catenary inflections in the sky, do not
say back to me
        what I say. When
fare and foliage run out, your half-
assed way withers to become
all you are. No, let me be
your callus, let us continuously
mislead one another
badly out of desire.

In the grey-locked docks, in the
colloquial consequence,
the resounding shame of having used language

    to pretend. I am not scared
of what is plain.
To be estranged was brought into
me this world, let me be yours.

Draped is my hand over the
flaw of your love, is worth the cold
true substance to my touch.

When what I feel does not
pertain to you, and pertains
to you still ... only then will I
leave your version of things, take cover
in the broadness of trees
in the angles of the moon.

                                    It doesn't work. I don't
anymore in the social mechanism of thought

I am always non-
            intellectually speaking

    wanting there to be something inside me
taken out

        gunmetal cradles my
    head despite it
            being hard
        to be happy
                even now

            passing as a child

unable to pluck myself off the tree

        state which limitations I feel

            one does not do
        nothing but everything

    to keep the stone and leaf pattern
            from dying their inner death

given, curiosity will not arrest

        I have tried
they will not   those poems of intelligence and new
        feeling

nor a ripped wave of time's hopeless honesty
mend this parted night

                              He will not do— it is
            you again I want

I do not know what it means
to brute up in my own fire

                bury twisted arms
                  adjoined under
                wet soil

against your body let mine
grow weak

        it has never even tried

my imagination is not dishonest

but attached

night is superfluous negation and in my sleep
I see men

        man is a form of my desire
                negligible
            without what I supply

to be put in one's place is also power

  when I touch your arm—what does
    it matter? I am not happier for
saying it   only that I can live out there

        I bring myself an available
world apart

for reasons other than "manhood," "womanhood,"
  things of others' making, I beg you:

                                                    take me from me

any less, I shall have to give myself over

       It's only a matter of time
before there's something, over
         these branches to lose   that I will not.
Leaves reach and turn, a body

             one can't know why but who is—
      What's the word for how you call
      the sea nearer? It's what's

      between us I've come in for. The
situation turns, on its own pleasure.
        You see me for what you are, like branches
      into snow, what I feel,

      becomes us. Here is
    snow. We will swim and scroll like
beads in a pack. You can't deny it

         though I'm used to you. I feel it as I've

always thought: per each count of
      passing winter, it was something:
It is the last thing to be moved to change.

Fringe sheets of mist carried off from
clumps of rain. If only you were
      to make me, go past and
make myself felt. To mirror,
the sun drowns in libations
      sky oversoaking the sauce.
What's not done is really meant tomorrow.
      No one at this time is here.
      You have branded with your voice
the immensity of my seclusion that dips and festers.
Like a hand you put on mine.
Ah, like a jacket. Cozy trees, makes
      a kind of reticence. Does my baby take
only agony? Intently upon me as it is
the aspen shakes abrasively, the
      only goosebumps
because I know what you did to me.

It's everything you do
I get to these days, comes around
to affect me.
The sound of friction is a joint endeavor.
From the shadowed cape of a ridge:
From part of the grass rose stone.

Once I see it I can't stop:
Something in the hard ground spring
clutches from their banality these moments,
raises this golden mixture to an invisible sky
of all prior despair.

Ice unfolds its clasp: it takes too little
to feel: destroy everything just to include
yourself, so as to find—
so fail
that it makes me real, with all the world
I do perceive and everything I don't.
In my eyes
it is emotional, pressed against the beginning of how the tone will
turn out with more to say.
If it's there, goes on
the horse: moss down the wall, leaves strapped on the Thames,

Exceedingly part of this surface of
physical time, there in space
Supposedly not ourselves

Narrowness spare us,
time through mountain-peaks from the hand of fall,
believe in these things less innate.
By themselves
things are necessary to me
item by item, round and round, as waves
grind to the shore, running low and steady
as a no-longer-young work—

Do I already regret today?   sleep
to have energy to sleep again?
Not by error but by the thawing frame reveal
grassy slopes, the late low-noise without permission
of things ticking off

Things I have no idea of
come to me
expressions as if unprecedented
because they stand, suddenly manmade, in the look of death. Green all year
then bright blood of trees, and the long distance view that hangs
eastward to the facade

Everything not in this which is, dares not take
our eyes off what remains

things I knew nothing about,
the weight, the sound of bombs
they came to me

Days take care, spending years
just being yourself in part,
making it known, as it perishes from definition
to take the inside of her cheek.
No one knows why
again. Sun rolls down the hill like a giant tear,
bonds weaken between branch and leaf and
light shoots through her the kinds of useless sound
solace isn't found in. I say, anything but
you instead of me, and see the water
flash off an eave like marbles.

The way things make sense
when they shouldn't. When amputations replace our lumps of half-snow,
randomness itself limping around without a neck.
The city, that is no longer perpendicular to her grave,
buildings on their knees where it's always day from bomb-light.

The way I see it, the parched tell me everything is fake water
something to look away from
when nobody should have to look that far.

things had I not heard
would not have conceived. out
of ways to say it, fucking
obviously, as they intentionally
hurt the children. what I have or
what I am when we move
in different circles. fate
of her favorite brush she lost
while the soldiers cheer. with time,
a full-length story. with felt and
metal I can't write of, get
specific about, or else

        what's within
reach?

whatever is leavened
albeit intensified. naturally
it comes up. what I do before
I know it for far less, then
I spread it, apart. the effect
lives in all honesty. snow
closes down on an interim, the sill
leavened with snow.

moon and sun at once
sun as pathetic as moon
as cavities of bush fill with
glistening white and squirrels
and where the stream still stirs,
the decay of sunlight
in a thousand steps.

whatever is leavened
comes down, fucked up,
is deeply involved. you
get chills just from how
it churns and thrives when
they remove your favorite
stone. lobbed, in a
pointless way I don't
feel like, on any day such
as this, the first straight thing
come to me.

the temptation to stay here
only is strong, but there is
flesh that is the trouble.
clouds overhead will tear
us apart, our sodden faces that
wished a certain build again. some
weakness in me to be, that
desire is strong. I
conform to time's way
of taking, carrying on the
rest of the speeding bunny
snow.

the unimaginable happening
exactly and my fingers are
left in the end with a video.
more times had I taken this
than my body would not have
me speak for it. and what does
not wilt in the land? and
who will have on hand
some water? put it like
an animal carefully forward.
having a mind for it
begins outstripping this, must
begin there. it has not
always been so educated
to not touch upon that world.

                say about. say
about. the promise
of discontent
is in what we have
just said. that will have us
not like the rest, squander it.

that you tell me some
part of it, isn't that
what it means to think
with a view to stay and
thus in every sense
faithfulness. this tide that
reveals we conceal, are
free but not intended
to know. and the midst
of night where day by you
is so soon there.

not always so. cut,
my hair would grow
but when I leave it's you
who's gone. what isn't
written, forced to live out,
marked as the under-belly
to every hour keep on.
thoughts, a mutant thing
and solace is gone too close
to me.

what I do not look for
and what I do, as if it were
myself. nothing
is always, for now is what
leads to all other things.
at the very least, the
tides are for their almost
forever change, there,
keeping with the view.
a tried and true, help-
lessly strong counter
to our attachment.

what I want to not fall
back on but with this, make
effort with the already
expressive nature, in
a sense, the meaning.
is it or is it not too late
to not become that
person, or in all political
likelihood, how slow
the fastness can go
versus, or that is, humane.

and is there forgiveness
in you for this, an interplay
with such parachutes
of beauty we inevitably
come down from. rebuild
a pure space, try together
to touch upon real things
nonetheless. as I articulate
myself no clearer
I must come out now
sounding contradictory,
loving in so strict
a sense. and how far

can one disagree the
test of acceptance against
growing solitary faith.
such questions of
our time. such questions
we hear asking us. there is now
and an end that reflects
how we imagined it. but
our feelings cannot be.
I say: what to do

with such forgiveness
of the unforeseeable? but
you say, *Jenn* come down.

off-blue morning sheets
that heightened sense.
sometimes I think
I'm to take all of it, strung
along by the memory
of an intensity.

cause me to dwell
in obscurity to you, make it
becoming of all-night.
even for me
I end up saying things,
to be at arm's length, high
in the name of a violent feeling

we do not burden it with
anything other than what
it's meant, that it is already for
what it needs to be. others
would make it work reasons
unjust until I can hardly
say why. I know
               you know
I've always wanted it as it
was, is evident in how it
leads me by my choice.
already it promises the
worth of undertaking it
our feelings, not unemployed.

said it's all the same
thus making it something
else entirely, lost to itself
and to that light earlier
than even day yet in a sense
there. when it is not
the same, not even the
impossibility of making obey
audible sound those thorns
out of snow.

link us with what is
hidden in the deep hard
snow. once one of us leaves
it gets harder to return
to what is here. to exist without
what we have come to
need to eliminate certain
forms of our desire. and
exempt even our past
from the weaponry
of this simplification.

most groundless of blue
shadows across snow, dunks
and seeps into the crumbs
of tempered shade. what
is it you want
from what you say? say *that*
instead, which has brought me
to you, as sudden as
unable to hide, in the thatch
of a fervor.

how much of it we at last
see does not suffer here
but does not share our past.
we cannot support it, even
as we want for that, to propel
or say: understanding be lost
from us once more
for the words. it must be
           moving enough
for us to go, that which
doesn't take all of me when
I want to speak but leaves some
to desire. much of it's so
brilliant we don't expect
under arborescent forces
to return when we go, or any
equivalent furtherance.

on a pull-out sofa bed, looking
past trees at scalloped ice
on the snack bar awning,
it hardly hurts to come apart
this way. you've given me
your poems and I've given
you mine.

there are some days and nights
when it doesn't seem I could
but am living for that.

now I don't want to come back
the other men in me I could
each mounting moment subject to.
and as I am smitten by personality
it becomes "a thing in my life," admiring
those students as I do. I do, judicious,
esoteric and a long run later
      into the arms of winter light.

fair failing, happy with the blood off this bone
I want for it only illimitable
weatherproof matrimony to my means.
lodged in a thought of me should you try
cagey   with the throng of its fount
to prosper, pierce me and blossom.
equipped with such flair we lift
      off one another, it's quite normal.

all that doing things with
our minds leaves me
far past wanting to know.
we cannot be who we were
hung and shed and hatchbacks
with their mohawks of
morning light. I can't
tell. no one wants to hear it
from me anymore.
           still, my present
to you: youth life. we met
just after that. what I know
or is it what I don't of you.
hoping now I never figure
some things out, how the
words in me press to sharpen
all the ways we don't.

other than us it won't be
as we were, but will not
cheat us of our defense.
so few ideas come for us
now, the chevron waves
pound into mangled snow.
one minute it's all possible.
the next, of course I
remember
          who you are.

the beginning doesn't
but I develop sexual
feelings. we who are too
quick to learn. lift up your
arms. I've started
seeking answers, not
questions, the propensity
to show you I can mean.

what we make of this
suppleness, or yesterday,
when what's between us
stays, long after and seems
important to articulate
such things before more
time passes—something a poet-
novelist once said,
to the most defenseless in me.

does the power flow
important to us how.
as the world's talent for
dying, keeps in brazen view.
or something to take over
when these thoughts, shiny
have passed, and you're
equipped to incorporate them
into this changing world.

only some of that holds
to the end of my feeling for
now. some of it's so
great-sounding it can be
as common as abused
youth. something outside
upon the snowy light.
something inside me, very
nauseous.

really, every other facet
does have something to say.
in bullshit and in great
brutality, it comes out
on the snow. I said I wouldn't,
but can remember sheltering
what penned a line in me
to no clear advantage.

he said, make it FAVORABLE
to which I'm claiming *yes*. we
who have borrowed
being. permit us become
true periphery. what's allowed to
will lift the cobbles
of love, if not incessantness.

and we mean too much
of what we say, and by
our words alone, come
to be known. the more
the sea the less we're
kept up on ordinary
ground. in the direction of
some further love, till it
has always also needed
some way to be.
              no way around
to cut it, what's from, but
isn't really you. I continue
in our attempt to be more
than us. more, this time,
more simply.
it's a radiant thing
we find ourselves up against.

the life this requires
and of us more fully
conceived, with no
faintheartedness but
what, however poorly
we would say. I'd rather
that than anything else
right now be said.
for such small change
takes all of winter, the
face
            of water
facedown and actuating
against the springbed's
baby baldness. a kind
of cognitive dissonance,
that we are changed by
what we agree is
impossible, or it's so
beautiful it cannot yet
must be. as I love
I will lose, all myself
in the uppermost regions
of your being there.

in what part of this we
deform as much as the
rest may stand. a sound
hardly out of reach
and going four, five
ways at once. to fully
exert, for and into this
is to be given back by it
so much more. why else
would we answer to
life, which so dauntlessly is
                what it's like.

Ode to Inexperience

what is actual, is
what we desire on.
gentle touching
actions, oneself into
being. without
pressuring the most
delicate of us into
reciprocity, also
occurs. we go out of
the way it was not
meant for us. to look
gotten, when what
is true is we desire
on.
                      it is joy
makes me splash
like pines up a cliff, long
divers of darkness
between thinking and
overthinking lose
their edges like stars
in their brightening.
it is desire, on her back,
trying to get results
another way. you are
so resplendent you
are not fit to lead.
you rupture, so
thoughtlessly, it plays
with my addiction to
this feral bastion of
petals. they collapse
inwardly, but open
like an ambassador.

for stars, to squirt up
pooling ruminations,
rain chucking sprung
halos on a creek.
demands of my being,
arise simply having
not been there. each
time, longing to start
from the farthest
position only, to
watch you come out of
around me. from us
I draw like the tensing
mind away, a kind of
life-pain, cold in me
till beaming. but how to
not rely for import on things
associated with you.
space cozies up, exhausting
the envelopes of stars
while size-wise, the
brightness is incredible,
wants to open small
inserts in my flesh.

without this levity, so
lillypadish, we'd surely
break, one another by
the dumb appearance
of what we're capable of.
all by us, an ardent
changeover, like a zamboni's
gentle defacing actions.
for love I don't get to,
leave but learn
to rely on what surrounds
me. it is joy, acquired by
congenital pain. do I
ever come to not
needing it, spinning
few contraptions just
to stay close to
reply. we get to where

we can't, having been
taught by the things in
each other.

grated snow, like
cardboard comes on
my face, violent but
painlessness—. the
torn pieces switch
between my lips like
they long for. it drifts
from an angle, this
feeling that's as much a
part of what can't be
apologized for, as
what can't, taken
seriously, come back
from us. the ways
to never stop. I've
known myself to try my
hair, wet on my head
like a dressing or a large
oozing leaf. all night

clasp and kind.
submission to, recompense
for, what's residually
enforcing expression. I
am needing it more. it
is wanting more. this
asymmetry is
                    fragility.
everything I encounter
becomes a thing to
send you to make of
it—truthfully, same. I
almost do not become
what I am, tomorrow.
these avant-flowers for
nobody by that name here
spontaneously, hang on.
but should you give me
the correct address, would

I not promise to deliver
them?

always changing outside
this, such that I want
to feel, a difference. I
would be that for you.
the thing affixed to an
old verity, different
when actually said. ant
tracks of light, adverts
on the sides of reflective
buses. five to six
minutes in, a farfetched
plenty honest fast-
barbed. I used to have
self-control. the
tenth elegy moves me
like treatment. just because

it doesn't come for me
as straightforwardly
doesn't mean it isn't
sleeting, and the rain
turning at present to
snow. where in this, can't
I cathect? where in this
do I say it's not hard, to
discover the ending or the
"real" subject. in here
I still get to see you,
change. right now
I feel enough of the way
I believe I should. it
is so you are able,
and come with. what
could be realer. we
leave behind what
        we say we can't.

what is equal to more
than can be said, to a tenderness
with its sharp
triangular handles: a kind of hyacinth
and yeast in her garden. *Look,*
it has spread to my neck, shoulder, and back
a thousand pieces of my
heart come to ascendence as a bear-shaped
pacific foam. this thing of yours
which changes but not enough, a terminology
of moaning as familiar to me
as childhood dynamics: *I can't alter*
my consciousness with consciousness. back-lit where
I go through nearby colossal trees
the extreme tenderness of voice with which she
speaks of you

softness continuous, to leave
    absence of, if only
the blue and green box. I feel nothing
    that doesn't matter
within. a dent of light, hot leaves flinch cinched
    but flicker like metal. so infer the time

shifting lost days in awe of detective work,
    the specificity joy takes
given form to hold up through shade
    the other side. in water feel quicken
perks up. I can see to where I
    can't get. it's okay, the group
everything comes in loses my place
    skilled motion in leaves holding out.

see the distance in the distance now
        it focuses on becoming this century
the water-like rock, the scarf. it won't do, is
        seen and done with whatever is
well to get rid of. if it completes you, suddenly

take it from me. under the sun mountains
        crumple. the part of me that wants to
die is strictly speaking there. branching
        shadows appear fallen on the roof.
up close I can never be content.

    Pancake ice pedals sunburnt
unsorted as sight may be. I dreamt it
      in complete silence
        the waterfall, where past it

    slush stations and diverts, trucking
downward water on night sky.
      It's so loud it could go
      either way. These things

    not dream nor water, but our own. I
worry about that. Principles harden
      the practice, things come out
      silent under the influence and it's

    so loud I'm part of how I'm
unsure. It's moving: whatever we take
      shape on, these modes of
      encouragement we can hardly

    but might resist. It passes before
you can parse the wrong from right
      ways of pain. And which way
      is past me? When this is culture.

        The world is crazy. All
around me lies the horizon.
            No sooner shall I be capable
of finding you than sky
                deteriorates love of sport.   I know

            what you're undergoing are merely
            words. It's a shame
love's not the truth, of who we are.
            To be out   thinking

            it   does not escape it.   So light
changes what does not.
            Beyond the field of present time, it's
reasonably commodious

            to come back. It's something I
haven't had, in a long time.
            Dusk between buildings exudes
a brilliant pink. What doesn't happen

            to me yet   I long to feel.
The ochre deepens we are sick of.
            Pines in a windlessness.

I would, or just take a long walk
by the same dream again. Where overgrown stitches
pull apart to reveal a fractured field of white,
your upper lip poking, then bristling against
what there is to.

                      Caliginous quibbles, dreams
best seen at night, reconstructed by touch
on all fours. Is there a lot
of blood? I confess
I see it that way, before I disappear and
everything is like the same, and everything
flows, outward now to be of lighter
touch, avoids making much pain or bliss
last beyond fleeting form.

Tell me something I can believe
will stay. For if I do, so should my hands
belong to us to touch this finite gift of space.
You permit me to use your name, give it up,
fed by winter's spring at a distance, our earliest
and our latest sleep...

                              Birds with flight
resist the funneling of life away. Fill me with
no bulletin of sorrow but help me. Put outside
we share an exterior, minutes
winding back death's authority. Whatever we had,
my fault was rigor where our logic knew no end.
Into night I hammer a moon-beam-ripple,
strides of light I see are my advantages—
        only for myself, to myself
  not just cast out the window.

Bound at present with no end, no *but,* is to be
impossible. With time that appears, it is time
you do. What actively-going factors
it is already saying to itself, like my earliest person I feared
to lose before all else, who could inspire hungering
for even more than was safe. Likened to this,
it was more care than rigor.
Tell me something I wouldn't believe.

Ísland

1.

whatever happens to that – that silence
between us I made so quietly
none see, snaking whispers, draped

meltwater on snowy stone as unevenly
sun falling enables floes to drift beneath
night-cuts, hours of vibrant pink, combing

fresh streaked mountains like meat above me.
no   whatever becomes of it, don't let it
become me, sorry and no fairer

not saying what I say

2.

out away once more of
desire, civil twilight, reshaping
negative space with a darkish
river from above. nothing pleases

me more, save those for oneself,
than feelings softly landing, the
snowflake breaking off its
arms in sun, hardening over
night the water of its spears

3.

forgive this greed for life, forbids me
from kissing any other, having never
stroked it before the sky-squeezed-out

sun, flat snouts of glaciers. out of
grotesque bedrock, long-nippled
spires glisten wet and the curve of

earth where darkness is morning. to black
sand plastered grasses evolve to clutch.
where gusts out-brood us stunning

stillness deafens.

4.

speak less, sing. may I

pass that term when

I do not see you yet

safely. I mention you

so often to myself it

seems I knew you by

the time I did. hence

how little I speak and

captivating you are

5.

then many more air cavities

depressed throw with altered

direction under slipped darts

of snow. down the mount

can't see, can't feel what's

sogged through to the leg. head

crusted with baby ice, just go,

don't look, peel off the frozen

pant, the boot, the glassy

thigh in the station bathroom

light. thoughtlessly wiped, alive

your body won't make tremor.

then fear flashing colorless

and the sudden reprieve: *that*

> *the mind's the only*

> *thing left moving*

6.

thoughts through mist through morning
bandaged clouds, hands twisted on the
basis of clouds. bird me, pluck me if

I'd let you. doffed murmurs possess fullness
society restrains, a sky of silence grows.
you are a tree in a new invasion of light

swaying in me towards acts beyond our
capacity. to you I communicate things only
quietude hears, but tread among pronounced
signs of ardor, flaring crocuses – the

way you began was outside me

7.

not what was and left but lingers.
all around flutters a strand of trees
near the time of death, so always.

cool air drives north waters wayward
rocks the rain to sleep and darker light.
incredible what doesn't go inside this
gets to hold it, and when longing gets long
you cut it like abandoning your mother's cart.
but obsession: this, too, lets the days go

8.

mother it is night
is life coming back for me

       there are no vendors

   I no longer dream the closest shave
all my adulthood I have been searching for
     a higher threshold of spirit

   let me side
with misers, spy
  the laundry shape
up in the wild

      out of the running, no wolves
      give birth
      that's me
      and my shadow foists its pitted hand into a stiffer
        hunger

compared to you
    mother
   what is night
      green patches
duck and pucker between
boards. I found

            myself a heart
         past what you know to do—from here,

I leave my stick behind
I bring our child into the hour of the grotto.

9.

grays shine out the quick den almost-black, taut
conical waves flooded with red beacons, removed from the foothills
of high mountains. perfection avoids temperature where
high and apparent is what moves that inner wind to come out and say
sentiment is metrical, not literary. the centerline moves against the space
between pavers. to have engaged in forbidden trades, learned that discipline
of rush and hunger. let what has its say
take effect, the dog in me does not swallow the crystals I give to it.
to start is unable to turn back; it is extremely difficult and thick in the air. we are
what we did to ourselves, the marks suggest we were there when
we were born. disappearance is depth relative to the iris, to see it moving
is to be let down into seeing what I do not gently.
fathom the clarity and brightness, what is done in every other street.
in this country, am I still responsible? I've never been
an islander for decades, shall be out
with a bag and knife sometime today.
      from the foothills in the distance
      five minutes is enough, and it is
      not if it is what
      regrows the light. the light
falls straight expensively soft pillowing among mantles, dry soil necessities.
there's no focus to what's past when points of inflection through the waves
may be too poetic. if something is to be unmanageable, needs it to be this, autistic as
waves talking over themselves, red bantering subtlety's gray

10.

climbing out the present, rippled

to the crust, exaggerated by the influence

of a gale, be small. fish abundant in the

fjord, and one so busy catching

did not make hay or love, yet do those

fish dance out from his eyes in winter, split

by fire

* * *

Tonight I have lost what
I was going to say

timothy, I have never seen such schizophrenic skies

waves violation

it won't relax
this hair
punching through the follicle

will I never attain the proper
disfigurement
to confess before the council?

my heart limps gorgeously

all day I stray from myself
towards a hiding place to glimpse
                             lightishness from

because I am sneaky, there is
no outcome to sex

        I let you go to your absence
is real enough for me

timothy, alexander
what is mine to wager
        I could pull on my platitudes thereby
changing your face

but I want you to make yourself
                        into an escape
bring to my mind what

your eyes fell to at sea

if we know each other well
       we will interchange
a semi-urban loneliness, whole years
       from diary sections

let us perfect a disconnection, misunderstand
our involvements completely

       cosmic pitches course through
       back-systems like mold in
             gouda

to find the truest I
       I cannot be

let me have my love to lose

       model my garments after seismic fonts

the trees are sculptures from experience

a capital O of dishwater on the belly of your shirt

       and it has taken my heart
       to be well. anyone who would like to but can't
          tells me something

the way inside is from the outside only

the day it will be more true, the obstacle of each speech, to life

you're the kind of beginning
       that doesn't spoil how it ends

on my bed's four legs
sleeping
    intentionally
  unsearchable there
            I am the compromise
            of all I am

                              such is the repair time passes
              for deep things

habits broken, then mended by fire

must I keep my old feelings in tact?

                              dark
                              bright greens return
                                        to the sides
                              of bare branches,   the switch

              has the effect of a
gradual dimmer

so easily coaxed are my thoughts like water, at the border
being held by you as if

              by grief. I am content
              others achieve
                              some passage in me. it is
technique

              to be all voice, no self, or
all the critics were wrong
              without hurt: this is my truest self. the lock

              is not moral ground, where I do not seem
              to coincide

all the content depends on what you are moved to consider

              the Anglepoise lamp as it arches back, or else

I've simply failed in my endeavors, and fall out of

              tense, the need to appear
imprecisely, being the one
              who changes

the background appears in gentle, monstrous force

I have courted in the north, seduced there my death. tell me,

shall I atone now with comfy, useless
                              words of life?

words are more than a series of simple maneuvers

the spiritual comes out in a sensuous manner

            I have glimpsed the length of your
        cycling coat. one should see to it

there are zigzags and squares. the actual

        is breathtaking.   it washes
dreams by hand and what for
                              am I already

a professional?

word is, if only it weren't so quiet
word is, I can't hear myself saying

this time of the year you are essential to me

        can you sense the pleasure of the person
who created it? can you meander
        in a huge loop so I can
deal, with this caked
        dread on my coat, have no right

feeling depressed?

my love for poets is practically non-physical

a small group of birthday children

a man on the canal yelling he's gonna kill whoever took his dog

a long brook and rebellion unexplored
                in my mind

            more than that
                whatever
        is inconsolable, pumping

    conditioner into its
own hand, or scrape

   back the hairs, come
    down, I can't get past
what those people said at me

I'm scared
  my eyes are up to
that tapering all my life
    into flatness

daily I have my pick of fat and crime
but not the
    forwardness I must

believe with, handsy
  in blindness
as if at some
    one

an article proposes a certain stress in the world

morning is still the gray night turns out to be

  long grained rain butters the air as
winds tailor water at my canoe

  my identity, a ruin darkness guards

     in this demeanor I could go on, past
      my impatience into forever—

   just in case
I have been here this whole time

the excitability of a pretty face, the sound

  of nothing eavesdropping

rather than a gothic heroine I'd be a happy slut

and this is how I professed to be a cobbler

with reverence toward my cutter
with use for my thread

None of this matters. It's only supposed
to save you from yourself. None of this
matters, when I try to take it out of me into
the world, which to find I can praise
                                  I go out to

My Earliest Person was written between late 2022 and early 2024. Some poems have previously appeared in projects by Face Press and *Folder*. My deepest thanks to those editors, and to Phil Baber, who so graciously took this project on.

To those who move me on a daily, monthly, yearly basis—who have given me my feelings and kept my desire at every stage and displacement of my life—this book is for you.

Copyright © 2025 by Jennifer Soong

Published by The Last Books, Amsterdam / Sofia

Designed and typeset by Phil Baber

Printed in the EU by Tallinn Book Printers

ISBN 978-9-49178-013-4